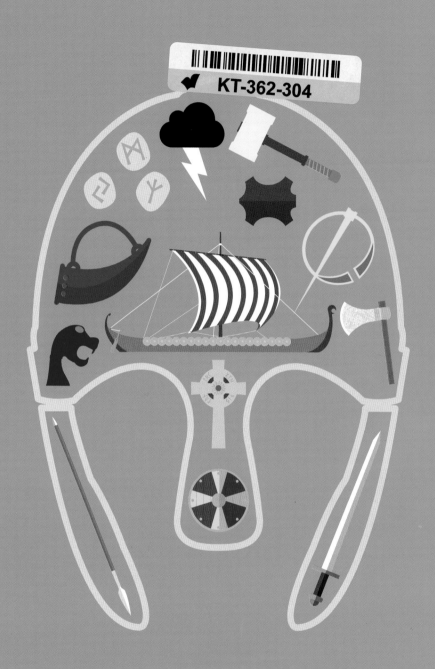

CONTENTS

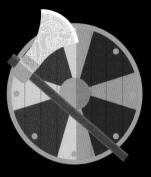

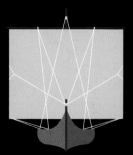

WELCOME TO THE WORLD OF INFOGRAPHICS

Using icons, graphics and pictograms, infographics visualise information in a whole new way!

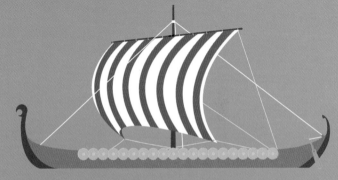

READ ABOUT HOW THE VIKINGS MADE THEIR FOOD TASTE BETTER.

FIND OUT WHICH VIKING GOD RODE AN EIGHT-LEGGED HORSE.

DISCOVER THE FAST SAILING SHIPS THAT VIKINGS USED TO CROSS THE OCEANS.

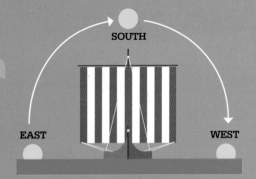

COMPARE A VIKING LONGHOUSE WITH A MODERN JUMBO JET.

FIND OUT HOW THE VIKINGS FOUND THEIR WAY ON LONG VOYAGES.

SOUTH

EAST

WEST

WHO WERE THE VIKINGS?

The Vikings were a group of people who lived in a part of northern Europe called Scandinavia. From the 8th century to the middle of the 11th century, their power and influence increased as they moved across northern Europe and beyond.

789 CE
FIRST RAID ON ENGLAND IS AT DORSET

841 CE
VIKINGS SETTLE IN IRELAND

980 CE
NEW VIKING RAIDS ON ENGLAND

991 CE
BATTLE OF MALDON

878 CE
ALFRED THE GREAT DEFEATS VIKING FORCES AT BATTLE OF EDINGTON

1017 CE
CNUT BECOMES KING OF ENGLAND, NORWAY AND DENMARK

800 CE

900 CE

1000 CE

1100 CE

793 CE
RAID ON LINDISFARNE ON ENGLAND'S EAST COAST

867 CE
YORK CAPTURED BY VIKINGS

937 CE
ENGLISH RETAKE LARGE AREA OF CENTRAL ENGLAND CALLED THE DANELAW

1000 CE
LEIF ERIKSSON DISCOVERS 'VINLAND'

1066 CE
VIKINGS DEFEATED AT BATTLE OF STAMFORD BRIDGE AND NORMAN INVASION OF ENGLAND

982 CE
ERIK THE RED FIRST EXPLORES GREENLAND

THE VIKING HOMELAND LAY IN MODERN SWEDEN, NORWAY AND DENMARK.

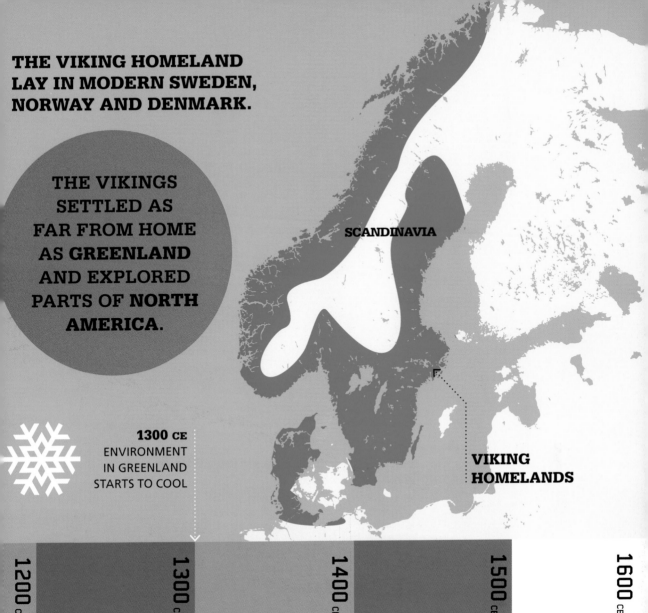

THE VIKINGS SETTLED AS FAR FROM HOME AS **GREENLAND** AND EXPLORED PARTS OF **NORTH AMERICA.**

SCANDINAVIA

VIKING HOMELANDS

1300 CE
ENVIRONMENT IN GREENLAND STARTS TO COOL

| 1200 CE | 1300 CE | 1400 CE | 1500 CE | 1600 CE |

1480–1500 CE
VIKING COLONY AT GREENLAND DISAPPEARS

The name **'Viking'** comes from the old Scandinavian word ***vikingr,*** meaning **pirate,** and refers to the raids they carried out on foreign cities and villages.

VIKING SOCIETY

Viking society was very structured, with a clear hierarchy in which everyone knew their place and role. At the top were the kings who led the community, while at the bottom were the slaves.

KING

Also called the *konugr*, he was usually the leader of the tribe or controlled a small area, rather than a whole country. Some kings were even war chiefs who didn't control any land.

FREEMEN AND FARMERS

Known as *karls*, these made up the vast majority of Viking society. They included craftsmen, farmers, merchants and landowners.

GENEROUS RULERS

Kings were expected to be great leaders and warriors, good speakers and generous with their food and drink, as well as clothes, weapons and gifts.

LAW AND ORDER

All parts of Viking society were governed by the 'Thing', a local assembly made up of freemen. It upheld the law, settled disputes and made political decisions.

NOBLES

Known as *jarls*, they controlled tribes and areas under the king's guidance.

THE VIKING ASSEMBLY IN ICELAND, KNOWN AS THE ALTHING, FIRST MET IN 930 CE AND IS TODAY THE OLDEST NATIONAL ASSEMBLY IN THE WORLD.

SLAVES

Thralls were usually captured during raids and taken back to the Viking homeland. This class also contained bondsmen, who were Vikings who couldn't pay a debt. They then had to work until the debt was paid off.

VIKING LONGHOUSE

Longhouses were important buildings to the Vikings. These long, thin structures were built for freemen to live in and they held everything Vikings needed for their day-to-day life.

PLAN OF A TYPICAL VIKING LONGHOUSE

FIRES
were lit in one large pit or several small fire circles. They provided light and heat and were also used for cooking.

WALLS
were made from stone, planks, logs or wattle and daub.

WATTLE AND DAUB
Wattle and daub was made by weaving strips of wood together. These were then covered with a mixture of soil, clay, sand and even dung mixed with straw.

1. Strips of wood are woven between upright wooden poles to create the lattice, or wattle.

Two rows of posts ran down the middle of the building, supporting the roof and dividing the room into a central area and two side corridors.

ANIMALS, including cattle and sheep, were sometimes kept in stalls at one end of the house.

ROOF might have been covered with turf or with straw and reed thatch.

BENCHES around the room provided seating.

SMOKE HOLES in the roof let the smoke out and some light in.

REEDS AND HERBS covered the earth floor.

BOEING 747 WINGSPAN
60 METRES

2. The mixture of mud, clay, dung and straw, known as the daub, was applied and left to dry to create a hard surface.

A LONGHOUSE WAS USUALLY
5 METRES WIDE
AND MEASURED UP TO
75 METRES
LONG – THAT'S WIDER THAN
THE WINGSPAN OF A JUMBO JET.

VIKING CLOTHES

Viking freemen and women wore simple clothes made from linen, wool and leather. The clothes were practical and designed to keep people warm during sea voyages and in the cold Scandinavian climate.

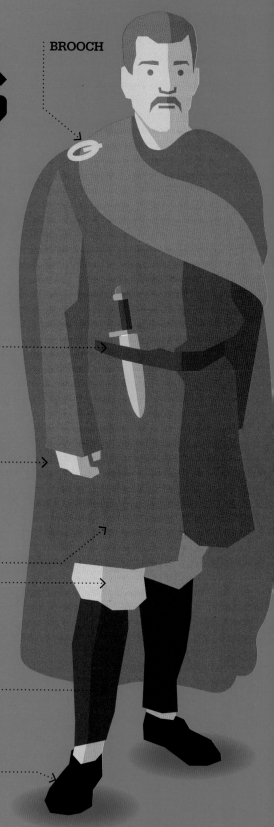

BROOCH

A **leather belt** held a sword, a dagger and even an axe.

A heavy **woollen cloak** kept the wearer warm in winter and was held in place with a brooch.

A **tunic** was worn over the **trousers** and gave protection from the harsh cold of a sea voyage.

Vikings wore trousers or **leggings** to keep their legs warm.

Shoes were made from leather and had hobnails hammered into the bottom to make the soles last longer.

The Vikings were keen on keeping clean. Archaeological digs have uncovered tweezers, razors, combs and ear cleaners.

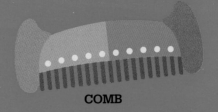

COMB

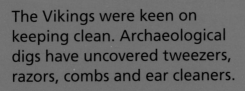

A linen **headdress** was worn over the hair.

Simple **jewellery** made from glass beads or amber may have also been worn.

Women wore long **dresses**.

Over the dress was a large **apron**.

RICH VIKINGS MAY HAVE WORN SOME CLOTHES MADE FROM SILK, WHICH THEY TRADED FROM THE FAR EAST.

VIKINGS COLOURED THEIR CLOTHES USING NATURAL DYES.

Blue was made from the woad plant.

Red was made from a small plant called madder.

Yellow was made from weld.

Vikings bathed **once a week** – Anglo Saxons at the time would only bathe **once or twice a year.**

52

2

VIKING CRAFTS AND CULTURE

The Vikings were very skilled craftsmen and women, creating objects that were used at home or traded abroad. They also created a rich culture based on long stories, called sagas.

FLAX

UPRIGHT LOOM

Most Viking homes had an upright loom to weave cloth from wool or a plant called flax.

RAW MATERIALS USED BY THE VIKINGS TO WEAVE CLOTH

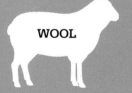

WOOL

A **turning beam** at the top wound the material as it was woven.

WARP THREADS RUN VERTICALLY

The **heddle rod** kept the warp threads apart so the weft threads could be woven through them.

WEFT THREADS RUN HORIZONTALLY

Weights at the bottom kept the warp threads tight.

WORDS AND LETTERS
The Viking alphabet was made up of 16 runes, as opposed to the 26 letters we use today.

ASCH	= A	HIS	= I	REHIT	= R
BIRITH	= B	GILCH	= K	SUHIL	= S
KHEN	= CH	LAGU	= L	TAC	= T
THORN	= P	MAN	= M	HUR	= U
EHO	= E	NOT	= N	HELAHE	= X
FEHC	= F	OTHIL	= O	HUYRI	= Y
GIBU	= G	PERCH	= P	ZIU	= Z
HAGALE	= H	KHON	= Q

The Vikings told long stories, called sagas, about their heroes and gods. These tales were memorised and passed from one storyteller to the next. They were not written down until the 12th or 13th centuries.

METALWORK AND JEWELLERY
Vikings were skilled metalworkers, making functional items, such as weapons and pots, as well as decorative jewellery from bronze or even gold.

Many Viking ornaments featured animals, especially twisting snakes.

SOME VIKINGS BURIED THEIR PRECIOUS OBJECTS TO KEEP THEM SAFE. THESE ITEMS COULD REMAIN BURIED IF THE VIKING WAS KILLED IN BATTLE OR FORGOT WHERE THEY HAD BEEN HIDDEN.

VIKINGS BAKED MEAT IN PITS FILLED WITH HOT ASHES. THE PITS WERE COVERED WITH TURF AND SOIL WHILE THE MEAT COOKED.

THE VIKINGS KEPT BEES FOR HONEY AND BEESWAX. THE HONEY WAS USED TO SWEETEN FOOD, SUCH AS SLOE BERRIES, WHICH HAVE A BITTER TASTE.

WEAPONS AND WARRIORS

The Vikings had a fearsome reputation as terrifying warriors. They fought using swords and axes and wore little or no armour to keep them as mobile as possible.

A Viking's weapons and armour reflected their social standing. Rich Vikings wore a **helmet** and a protective shirt made of **chain-mail**, and carried a **shield** and a **sword**, while a normal freeman used a **spear** and **shield**, with a **small knife.**

Axes carried by important people were decorated to show off their power.

SMALL KNIFE

SPEAR

Bows and arrows were used only at the start of a battle as they were thought to be less honourable than hand-to-hand weapons.

HORNS
Viking helmets did not have horns on them – this was a myth created in the 19th century. But this hasn't stopped people using the story. The Minnesota Vikings American football team wears purple helmets with horns painted on the sides.

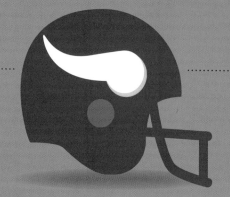

Viking **helmets** were made from leather or iron.

Some had a strip to protect the nose, or flaps around the cheeks.

A round **shield** was made from planks of wood that were fixed together.

Vikings carried a **double-edged sword.** They often gave their swords names.

Chain-mail was made out of small metal hoops that were linked together.

While many Viking actions involved small raids, the Vikings were involved in several major battles with large armies.

Battle of Maldon (991 CE) – up to 6,000 Viking warriors

Battle of Fulford (1066) – up to 10,000 Viking warriors

Siege of Paris (885–886 CE) – up to 40,000 Viking warriors

15

VIKING SHIPS

The Vikings used different types of vessel for different purposes, from small rowing boats to large, fast longships. They used these craft to fish, raid, explore and cross huge oceans in search of new places to live.

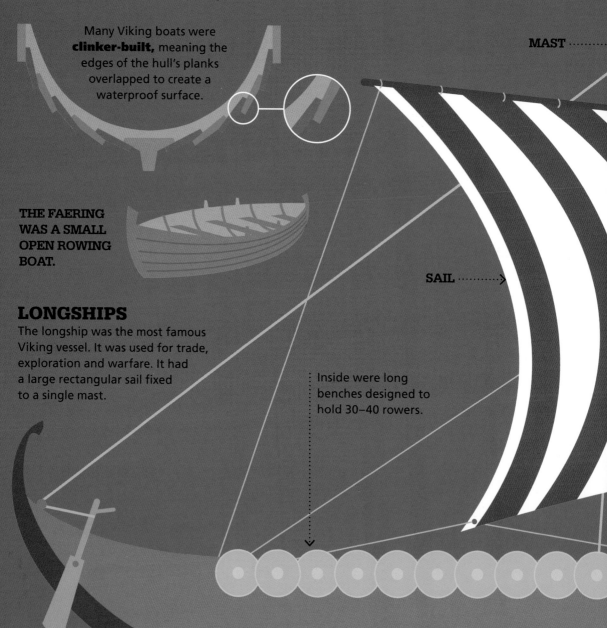

Many Viking boats were **clinker-built,** meaning the edges of the hull's planks overlapped to create a waterproof surface.

MAST ··········

THE FAERING WAS A SMALL OPEN ROWING BOAT.

LONGSHIPS
The longship was the most famous Viking vessel. It was used for trade, exploration and warfare. It had a large rectangular sail fixed to a single mast.

SAIL ·········>

Inside were long benches designed to hold 30–40 rowers.

The largest longships could

The knarr was a large vessel used for long sea journeys. The hull was wider, deeper and shorter than a longship and measured about **16 metres long and 5 metres wide.**

It could carry more than 40 tonnes of crew and cargo – greater than the weight of six elephants.

A KNARR HAD A CREW OF 20–30 SAILORS AND COULD COVER ABOUT 120 KILOMETRES IN A SINGLE DAY.

A longship was light enough for the crew to lift out of the water and carry over narrow strips of land. It could even be turned upside-down to create a temporary shelter.

Longships were also known as **dragonships** to the English, because of the dragons' heads carved into their prows at the front. These were designed to protect the crew and scare off sea monsters.

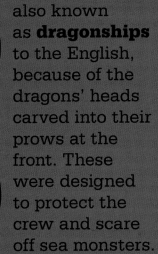

Its double-ended design meant that it did not have to turn around, making it very manoeuvrable.

LONGSHIPS COULD REACH A TOP SPEED OF ABOUT 10–15 KNOTS.

carry **100 Viking warriors.**

EXPLORATION

The Vikings were excellent sailors and they used their skills and tools to cross huge stretches of ocean. They even managed to reach North America, making the journey nearly 500 years before Christopher Columbus.

Greenland was first explored in the 980s CE.

VIKING EXPLORATION ROUTES

GREENLAND

NORTH AMERICA

The Viking explorer **Leif Ericsson** had the nickname 'Leif the Lucky' because he never got lost. Leif sailed for America around 1000 CE.

VINLAND (NEWFOUNDLAND)

Erik the Red was expelled from Iceland after several fights and killings. He then sailed on to **Greenland**, exploring the land. After three years Erik returned, claiming the land was fertile. He called it 'Greenland' to attract new settlers.

The Vikings called America **Vinland, or 'Wine-land',** after they found grapes and berries growing there.

ATLANTIC OCEAN

NAVIGATION TECHNIQUES

The Vikings used the sun as a reliable compass. It showed east at sunrise, south at midday and west at sunset.

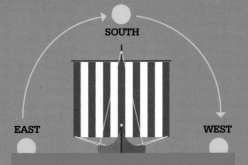

When it was cloudy, Vikings used a special crystal, called a **sunstone**, to work out the position of the sun.

Iceland was first spotted in 861 CE when **Naddod**, a Viking who lived in the **Faroe Islands**, spotted land after being blown off course on a trip west from Norway. He called the new land **'Snowland'**.

Vikings also used the **Pole Star**, or North Star, to tell which way was north.

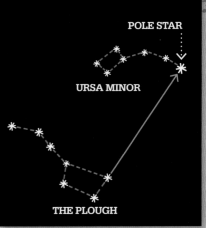

ICELAND

FAROE ISLANDS

SHETLAND

NORWAY

SWEDEN

DUBLIN · YORK

LONDON ·

CONSTANTINOPLE ·

RAVENS AND FLEAS

Viking sailors used to release ravens while out at sea. The ravens would fly towards land, showing the Vikings the right direction. Vikings believed that fleas always hopped to the north, so they would check their own fleas to guess the direction they needed to go.

TRADE OR RAID?

Viking ships carried warriors across oceans to raid and pillage foreign settlements. Their ships also carried merchants over huge distances to trade in goods from around the known world. And sometimes those same ships were used both to trade and to raid.

Viking traders carried small, portable scales around with them so they could accurately weigh out gold to trade with.

VINLAND

NORWAY – TIMBER, IRON, SOAPSTONE, WHETSTONES, BARLEY, TAR

GREENLAND – WALRUS IVORY, FUR, SKINS, WOOL

VINLAND (NORTH AMERICA) – TIMBER

ICELAND – FISH, WOOL, ANIMAL FAT, SULPHUR AND FALCONS

BYZANTIUM (CONSTANTINOPLE) – SILKS, FURS, SPICES, WINES, GEMSTONES, SILVER, JEWELLERY

FRANKISH KINGDOMS
– WEAPONS, JEWELLERY, WINE, GLASS, SALT, WOOL

Trading rates were usually set by local chieftains. For example, in 11th-century Iceland trading rates were:

8 OUNCES OF SILVER =	• 1 ounce of gold • 4 milk cows • 24 sheep • 72 metres of woollen cloth
12 OUNCES OF SILVER =	• one adult male slave

EAST BALTIC REGION
– AMBER, SLAVES, FURS

SHETLAND ISLANDS – SOAPSTONE

ENGLAND – TIN, WHEAT, HONEY, WOOL, BARLEY, LINENS

RUSSIA – SLAVES, FURS, HONEY

SWEDEN – IRON, FURS

SETTLING ABROAD

During the 300 years of the Viking Age, the Vikings spread out from their homelands and settled in lands across the North Atlantic, as far away as America. They also reached south to settle in large parts of Britain and Ireland as well as northern France and southern Italy.

VIKING HOMELAND

SETTLED LANDS

GREENLAND

NORTH AMERICA

In 1960, Archaeologists found Viking remains at L'Anse aux Meadows in Canada. It is the only known Viking site in North America and the earliest sign of European settlement on the continent.

200,000

The approximate number of people who left Scandinavia and settled in new Viking lands during the Viking Age

NORTH AMERICA

THE VIKINGS TOOK PLANTS AND ANIMALS WITH THEM FOR FARMING.

IT IS THOUGHT THAT ABOUT 90 OF THE 400 PLANTS LIVING ON THE FAROE ISLANDS WERE BROUGHT IN BY VIKING SETTLERS.

MOVING SOUTH

Swedes, known as Varangians, moved south and east through what is now Russia and the Baltic states. They reached as far as the Caspian Sea and Constantinople.

ICELAND

THE AREA OF BRITAIN SETTLED BY THE VIKINGS WAS KNOWN AS **DANELAW.**

SCANDINAVIA

BRITAIN

After defeating the Vikings in battle in 878 CE, the English king Alfred the Great made peace with the Vikings, allowing them to settle in the north and east of Britain.

BRITAIN

ITALY

Vikings raided parts of southern Italy during the 800s CE. In the first half of the 11th century, a Norman army conquered parts of Sicily and southern Italy.

FRANCE

From about 790 CE, Viking raiders began to attack areas in northern France. After a while they started to settle in the area, expanding their territory.

THE NAME OF THIS REGION, **NORMANDY,** COMES FROM THE TERM **'NORSE-MEN'** REFERRING TO THESE ATTACKERS FROM THE NORTH.

VIKING BELIEFS

Little is known about how the Vikings worshipped their gods. However, we do know a lot about the gods themselves, and the worlds they lived in, from the stories the Vikings told. Towards the end of the Viking period, this large group of gods was replaced by Christianity.

VIKING MYTHOLOGY DIVIDED THE COSMOS INTO THREE LEVELS.

The first level is **Asgard.** This was the home of the gods.

Bifrost, also known as the Rainbow Bridge, connected Asgard and Midgard.

Midgard, or 'Middle Earth', was the realm of humans.

VALHALLA

Valhalla was a huge hall where the souls of dead warriors were taken by mythical female warriors, called the Valkyries, to feast and drink.

Niflheim

Muspelheim

Below this were various realms, including **Niflheim** (the World of Fog and Mist) and **Muspelheim** (the Land of Fire).

THE NORSE GODS AND GODDESSES

Odin was the ruler of the gods.

He was the god of magic, poetry and war.

He only had one eye.

He rode an eight-legged horse called Sleipnir.

Freya was the goddess of love and fertility.

She had a twin brother called Freyr.

She wept tears of gold when she was unhappy.

Thor ruled the skies, storms and thunder.

He wore iron gloves and had a hammer called Miollnir.

Loki was the 'trickster god'.

He caused the death of Odin's son, Baldr.

He was a shape-shifter and appeared as a salmon, horse, seal and a fly.

THE GODS FOUGHT BATTLES AGAINST THEIR ENEMIES, THE GIANTS. THE VIKINGS BELIEVED THAT THE WORLD WOULD END WITH **A HUGE FINAL BATTLE,** CALLED **RAGNAROK...**

... A FIRE WOULD SWEEP ACROSS EARTH, DESTROYING MOST OF THE PEOPLE AND GODS, BUT LEAVING JUST A FEW TO SURVIVE.

Christian missionaries started to preach to the Vikings from about 700 CE. By about 950 CE, the Danish king **Harald Bluetooth** had been christened.

VIKING BURIALS

Viking dead were buried with artefacts, or grave goods, that reflected their standing in the living world. As such, Viking graves have been a valuable source of information to archaeologists about everyday Viking life.

THE AMOUNT OF GRAVE GOODS DEPENDED ON A PERSON'S SOCIAL STATUS

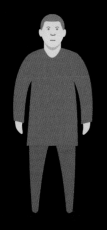

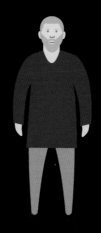

SLAVES
were usually buried in a simple pit, with no grave goods.

FREEMEN
and craftsmen were buried with their weapons and tools.

WOMEN
were buried with their domestic equipment and jewellery.

RULERS
and important people were buried inside wagons or even ships. They were also sometimes buried with a favourite horse or dog.

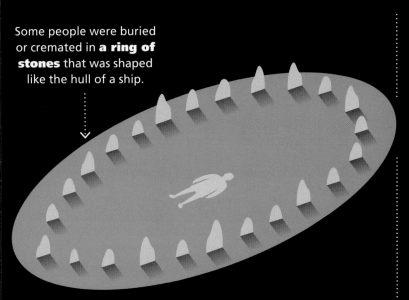

Some people were buried or cremated in **a ring of stones** that was shaped like the hull of a ship.

The largest ring found measures **170 metres long** – more than one-and-a-half times the length of a football pitch.

Many important people were **buried with slaves** who were sacrificed, possibly to serve their master in the afterlife.

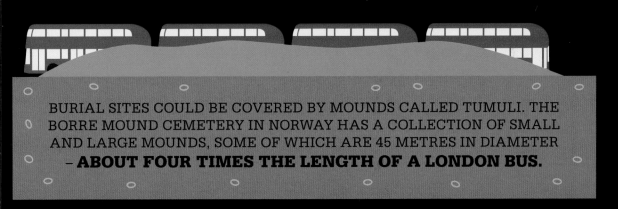

BURIAL SITES COULD BE COVERED BY MOUNDS CALLED TUMULI. THE BORRE MOUND CEMETERY IN NORWAY HAS A COLLECTION OF SMALL AND LARGE MOUNDS, SOME OF WHICH ARE 45 METRES IN DIAMETER – **ABOUT FOUR TIMES THE LENGTH OF A LONDON BUS.**

CREMATION WAS THE MOST POPULAR FORM OF FUNERAL DURING THE VIKING AGE. HOWEVER, THIS WAS REPLACED WITH BURIAL AS THE VIKINGS TURNED TO CHRISTIANITY.

WHAT HAPPENED NEXT?

Over time, the number of Viking raids declined. Viking territories started to unite under more powerful kings and rulers. Today, their influence can still be seen in many of the place names throughout their territory.

In 1013, **Sweyn Forkbeard** led a Danish invasion of England, forcing the English king, Ethelred the Unready, to flee. Sweyn became the first Danish king of England. He was succeeded by his son, Cnut, in 1014.

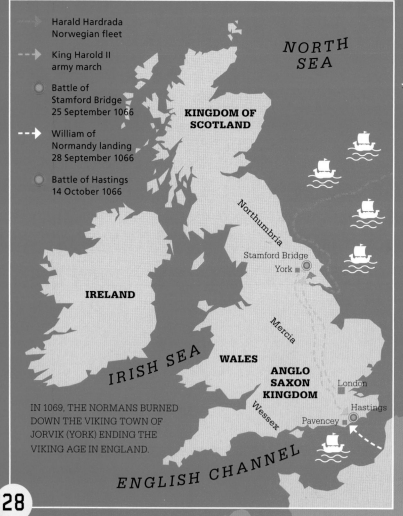

- ⟶ Harald Hardrada Norwegian fleet
- ⇢ King Harold II army march
- ◯ Battle of Stamford Bridge 25 September 1066
- ⇢ William of Normandy landing 28 September 1066
- ◯ Battle of Hastings 14 October 1066

NORTH SEA

KINGDOM OF SCOTLAND

Northumbria

Stamford Bridge
York

IRELAND

Mercia

IRISH SEA

WALES

ANGLO SAXON KINGDOM

London

Wessex

Hastings

Pavencey

ENGLISH CHANNEL

IN 1069, THE NORMANS BURNED DOWN THE VIKING TOWN OF JORVIK (YORK) ENDING THE VIKING AGE IN ENGLAND.

In 1066, **Harald Hardrada** led a Viking army in an invasion of England. He was defeated at the Battle of **Stamford Bridge** by a Saxon army led by **King Harold II** on 25 September. Harold had marched his army more than **320 km** in four days from London to Yorkshire. Harold then had to march **430 km** down to Hastings to face a Norman army led by **William of Normandy** at Hastings on 14 October. William defeated Harold, establishing Norman rule over England.

SPREADING INFLUENCE

Having settled in northern France, the Normans expanded their territory, conquering regions in **Britain**, **Sicily** and **southern Italy**, **northern Africa** and, during the Crusades, modern-day **Syria**.

PLACE NAMES

Many towns and cities are still known by their Viking names:
"**by**" meaning farm or homestead – **Derby, Whitby**
"**thorpe**" meaning farms – **Scunthorpe, Grimethorpe**
"**toft**" meaning site of a house or building – **Lowestoft**
"**kirk**" meaning church – **Ormskirk**

ENGLAND

Rouen
NORMANDY

Neapol   Apulien
          Kalibrien
Tunis   Sizilien
          Tripolis

Antochia
Latakia

SETTLED LANDS

Historians have put forward several theories about the decline in Viking raids and expansion. One theory is that European lands joined to **form large nations** with armies **better at defending** against **Viking attacks**.

THE CONVERSION OF MANY **VIKINGS** TO **CHRISTIANITY**, AND ITS PEACEFUL TEACHINGS MAY ALSO HAVE CAUSED A DECLINE IN VIKING RAIDS.

ANOTHER THEORY IS THAT A FALL IN TEMPERATURES CREATED A MINI ICE AGE THAT MAY HAVE DRIVEN VIKING SETTLERS FROM GREENLAND IN THE 1400s.

GLOSSARY

Althing
The name of the Icelandic parliament. It was established by the Vikings in 930 CE, making it the oldest national assembly in the world.

amber
The fossilised remains of tree sap. It is yellow or light brown in colour and is used to make ornaments and jewellery.

archaeological dig
The excavation of a historical site to uncover remains and artefacts that were buried many years ago.

Asgard
The home of the Viking gods.

bondsman
A person who is committed to performing an act for another, sometimes to repay a debt.

chain-mail
A type of armour that is made from small loops of metal that are interlocked with each other.

clinker-built
A method of building the body or hull of a ship where the planks of wood overlap each other.

cremation
A type of funeral where the body of the dead person is burnt to ashes.

dye
A substance that is used to change the colour of a material or hair.

flax
A type of plant, fibres from which can be woven to produce a material.

grave goods
Objects, such weapons and jewellery, that are buried with a dead person, sometimes in the belief that they will be used in the afterlife.

hobnail
A short nail with a large head that was hammered into the soles of shoes to make them last longer.

longhouse
The name of a Viking dwelling, the shape of which was long and thin.

loom
A device used to weave fibres together to produce cloth.

Midgard
The Viking name for the region where humans lived.

mythology
The collection of tales and stories, usually relating to gods and goddesses.

Pole Star
The star that sits directly over the North Pole. In the northern hemisphere, it can be used to tell where North is.

portable
Something that can be carried around easily.

prow
The front, or bow, of a ship or boat.

runes
The name given to characters used to spell out Viking words.

soapstone
A type of stone that is easy to sculpt and shape and used to make ornaments and jewellery.

sunstone
An almost transparent stone that was used to tell the direction of the sun on a cloudy day.

Thing
The name given to a Viking assembly to settle disputes and discuss laws.

tumulus
A large mound of earth that was placed over a burial site.

Valhalla
The Viking feasting hall where warriors went to drink and feast after they were killed in battle.

wattle and daub
A building material where clay, mud or dung (the daub) was smeared over woven sticks (the wattle) to produce a wall.

whetstone
A stone that is used to sharpen knives.

longship
A long, thin sailing ship used by the Vikings on long voyages and raiding expeditions.

INDEX

ACKNOWLEDGEMENTS

First published in Great Britain
in 2016 by Wayland
Copyright © Hodder and Stoughton Ltd, 2016
All rights reserved

Editor: Elizabeth Brent
Produced by Tall Tree Ltd
Editor: Jon Richards
Designer: Jonathan Vipond

ISBN: 978 1 5263 0024 9
10 9 8 7 6 5 4 3 2 1

Wayland
An imprint of Hachette
Children's Group
Part of Hodder and Stoughton
Carmelite House
50 Victoria Embankment
London EC4Y 0DZ

An Hachette UK Company
www.hachette.co.uk
www.hachettechildrens.co.uk

Printed and bound in China

The website addresses (URLs) included in this
book were valid at the time of going to press.
However, it is possible that contents or
addresses may have changed since the
publication of this book. No responsibility
for any such changes can be accepted by
either the author or the Publisher.

GET THE PICTURE!

Welcome to the world of **infographics!** Icons, pictograms and graphics create an exciting form of data visualisation, presenting information in a new and appealing way.

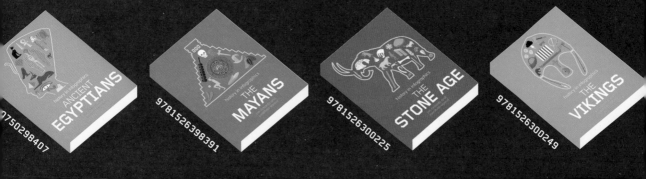